Need to Know

Depression

Claire Wallerstein

www.heinemann.co.uk/library

Visit our website to find out more information about **Heinemann Library** books.

To order:

 Phone 44 (0) 1865 888066

 Send a fax to 44 (0) 1865 314091

 Visit the Heinemann Bookshop at www.heinemann.co.uk/library to browse our catalogue and order online.

Produced by Roger Coote Publishing
Gissing's Farm, Fressingfield, Suffolk IP21 5SH, UK

First published in Great Britain by Heinemann Library, Halley Court, Jordan Hill, Oxford OX2 8EJ, part of Harcourt Education.
Heinemann is a registered trademark of Harcourt Education Ltd.

Editorial: Katie Orchard
Design: Jane Hawkins
Picture Research: Lynda Lines
Consultant: Christina Thompson
Production: Viv Hichens

Originated by Ambassador Litho Ltd
Printed and bound in China by South China Printing Company

ISBN 0 431 09809 3
07 06 05 04 03
10 9 8 7 6 5 4 3 2 1

British Library Cataloguing in Publication Data
Wallerstein, Claire
  Depression. - (Need to know)
  1.Depression, Mental - Juvenile literature
  2.depressed persons - Juvenile literature
  I.Title
  362.2'5

Acknowledgements
The Publishers would like to thank the following for permission to reproduce photographs:
AKG London pp. 11 (Erich Lessing), 27; Associated Press p. 30 (Shawn Baldwin); Camera Press p. 25; Corbis p. 13 (Kevin Fleming); Corbis Stock Market *front cover* (Cameron), p. 28 (Charles Gupton); John Birdsall Photography p. 40; Network Photographers p. 50 (W. Schmitz/Bilderberg); Photofusion pp. 5 (Paul Baldesare), 29 (Ute Klaphake), 32 (Paul Doyle), 37 (Christa Stadtler), 38 (Paul Baldesare), 45 (Paul Baldesare); Popperfoto pp. 9, 17, 20; Rex Features pp. 7 (Andrew Testa), 12 (Berry Bingel), 18 (Facelly), 26 (Fotos International), 34; Science Photo Library pp. 4 (Jim Varney), 22 (Alfred Pasieka), 23 (S. Cinti/CNRI), 33 (L. Willatt, East Anglian Regional Genetics Service), 35 (Mauro Fermariello), 39 (Geoff Tompkinson), 44 (CC Studio), 47 (John Griem), 48 (Jim Wvinner); Still Pictures pp. 15 (Sean Sprague), 19 (Ron Giling); Topham Picturepoint pp. 8 (Image Works), 10, 42.

Any words appearing in the text in bold, **like this**, are explained in the Glossary.

Contents

Depression

Marilyn Monroe, one of the most glamorous movie idols of all time, seemed to have it all – fame, beauty, money, and a string of handsome husbands and boyfriends. However, she suffered from one of the world's most common illnesses – depression. By the early 1960s, Monroe was under the almost constant care of a **psychiatrist**. She was also taking huge amounts of drugs to fight off the feelings of gloom, despair and low self-esteem that tormented her. In 1962 she committed **suicide**, at the age of 36.

A common condition

Experts say that up to one-third of us will suffer from depression at some point in our lives, and women are affected twice as often as men. One person in twenty is depressed at any one time. It is not only adults who suffer from this illness. Young people get depressed, too. In fact, depression now seems to hit more of us, and at a younger age, with every generation that passes. The reasons for this are not fully understood.

For people who have never suffered from depression, the condition can be very hard to understand. Depression can make people lose the will and energy to do even simple things, such as getting out of bed. Depressed people are more likely than the general population to get sick, have accidents, and not eat or sleep properly. In severe cases, they are also more likely to take their own lives.

Depression is already the cause of almost 30 per cent of all days taken off work. Experts at the World Health Organization (WHO) predict that depression will be the world's second-leading root cause of death by 2020. Despite this, it is thought that doctors may fail to diagnose around half of all cases of depression. Many people are too embarrassed to talk about their problems or seek treatment. Instead they may suffer in silence for years. This is a shame, because in most cases depression can be treated.

"I looked around me at the other people on the bus. I couldn't understand how the older ones could possibly have got to the age they had, as life was so terrible. Every day was an ordeal."

(Anonymous depression sufferer, quoted in the book *Depression* by Professor Edzard Ernst)

What is depression?

Depression is a very difficult condition to define. It is often referred to as the 'common cold of **psychiatry**' because it seems to be so widespread. Even animals seem to get depressed in some situations.

The word 'depression' does not just describe one illness, but various conditions. These range from the natural sadness we feel, for example after a loved one dies, through to major depression, which is usually caused by chemical imbalances in the brain.

How does it feel?

Many sufferers say that having depression is like living inside a grey fog or feeling numb all the time. Some depressed people may cry a lot, stop caring about how they look and seem very tired. Others may put on a brave face so the people around them have no idea that there is anything wrong.

People with what is called **manic depression** may sometimes seem like the most confident and lively people in the world – the 'life and soul of the party'.

In one very unusual kind of depression, known as Cotard's **delusion**, sufferers are convinced they are actually dead and no longer have any organs inside their bodies. People with this condition may even try to kill themselves to 'prove' to others that they are dead.

Diagnosing depression

Unlike more obvious illnesses such as measles, which makes the patient come out in red spots, there is no easy way to diagnose depression. Doctors use a checklist of more than 50 symptoms, at least six of which must have been overwhelming for more than two weeks. Some of the most common symptoms include **insomnia** (inability to sleep) or sleeping too much, being unable to enjoy things that were once fun, overeating or losing weight, inability to make decisions, extreme loss of energy, feelings of guilt, and, in severe cases, frequent thoughts of death or **suicide**.

"Schedule-wise, my health and peace of mind weren't a priority …
On the one hand, I was expected to be overjoyed by it, and at the same time I was disillusioned by it.**"**

(Canadian singer, Alanis Morissette, shown right, who started to feel depressed while touring to promote her album *Jagged Little Pill*)

What is depression?

Types of depression

Until recently, **psychiatrists** believed that depression was either 'endogenous' (coming from inside) or 'reactive' (reacting to events in a person's life, such as unemployment, divorce or stress). We now know that the causes of depression are more complicated than this. Since 1994, depression has been classified using a more accurate system called DSM4 (a guide for doctors produced to help them diagnose mental disorders such as depression more accurately). Some of the main categories are major depressive disorder, **manic depression**, substance-induced **mood disorder** and **dysthmia**.

Major depressive disorder (MDD)

Major depressive disorder (MDD) is also known as a mood disorder, or **affective disorder**. MDD is twice as common in women as it is in men. Without treatment, MDD lasts around nine months to a year. Some sufferers may not be able to continue to work or look after themselves properly. In severe cases they may even become obsessed with thoughts of **suicide**.

Manic depression

Manic depression is a kind of MDD. However, when sufferers start to recover from the lows of depression, instead of returning to 'normal', they enter an episode of mania.

Stressful events, such as school exams, may spark a bout of depression.

They may be incredibly happy and energetic, or find it hard to calm down, be very easily irritated and have signs of **psychosis**. Psychosis is a term used when someone suffers from **hallucinations** (seeing or hearing things that are not really there) and **delusions** (becoming totally convinced of something that is untrue). Manic depression is quite a rare condition – it only affects around 1 per cent of the world's population. It is sometimes called **bipolar disorder** because of its two changing moods ('bi' means 'two' in Latin). Depression alone is called **unipolar disorder** ('uni' means 'one') because it just involves one mood – low and bleak.

Drugs such as heroin may make users feel good for a while. But it is likely to make them depressed over the long term.

Substance-induced mood disorder

Substance-induced mood disorder is depression brought on or made worse by using alcohol or drugs. These substances affect levels of important chemicals in the brain – especially if a person has been using them for a long time and has become **addicted**.

Dysthmia

The term 'dysthmia' comes from the Greek word meaning 'bad state of mind'. The symptoms are similar to, but not as bad as, those of MDD. Sufferers can usually carry on with a fairly normal life, but the condition may last for at least two years.

Depression throughout history

Depression has always existed. As long ago as 1600 BCE the Ancient Egyptians used plant remedies to treat people suffering from depression (or '**melancholia**'). Later, ancient Greek and Roman doctors recommended remedies such as poppy extract and asses' milk, as well as gymnastics, massage and baths.

By the Middle Ages in Europe, treatment for depression had become more barbaric. It was a common belief that depression sufferers and people with other mental illnesses were possessed by evil spirits. They were often tied up or locked away in prison-like **lunatic asylums**.

In the 19th century, there was a big increase in numbers of people with depression. This was the time of the Industrial Revolution, when millions of people moved away from the countryside to overcrowded, polluted cities. The French **sociologist** Emile Durkheim blamed this breakdown in traditional lifestyles for the rise in stress, anxiety and depression.

Depression can become more common during times when life is harder for everyone. In the 1930s many people became depressed during a period of

In the past, many asylums for the mentally ill were violent and frightening places.

high unemployment and poverty known as the Great Depression. (The word 'depression' can refer to a downturn in the economy as well as in a person's state of mind.)

Early treatments

The first **antidepressants** were not developed until the late 1950s. Until then, the only medicines on offer were drugs called 'pep pills'. These could rapidly lift a person's mood. However, a short while later the person would crash into a severe 'downer'. Pep pills were also **addictive**. Some desperate people resorted to quite drastic surgery, such as **lobotomies**, in the hope of a cure. In a lobotomy operation surgeons separate the frontal lobes of the brain – the part responsible for a person's emotions – from the rest of the brain.

> **❝There is no happiness in life, only occasional flares of it.❞**
>
> **(Leo Tolstoy, author of the epic novel, *War and Peace*, who was a depression sufferer)**

Famous sufferers

Many historical figures have suffered from depression, including the US president Abraham Lincoln, who called his depression 'the shadow of madness'. Winston Churchill, the British prime minister during the Second World War, coined the phrase 'black dog' to describe his own illness. Sigmund Freud, the inventor of **psychoanalysis**, who treated hundreds of depressed patients, was a sufferer, too.

Lobotomies were a very drastic treatment – patients were left without any kind of emotional feeling at all.

Who suffers from depression?

Depression can strike people from all backgrounds. However, statistically, some groups of people are more likely to suffer from depression than others. Some countries have higher than average rates of depression. For example, in former Soviet countries life has become difficult since the collapse of **Communism** in the early 1990s, resulting in high levels of unemployment, crime and poverty. Today, nine out of the ten countries with the highest **suicide** rates in the world are in Eastern Europe.

People working in some professions seem more likely to suffer from depression. Usually these are people such as teachers, farmers and doctors, doing high-pressured jobs, working long hours or dealing with very sick people.

Poor people seem to be more at risk from the illness than rich people. They may have more problems, such as unemployment and money worries, that can trigger depression.

People doing tough and stressful jobs far away from home, such as these oil-rig workers, may be at greater risk from depression.

Feeling 'cut off' from society

People living in the countryside may suffer depression more than people living in cities. Poverty, lack of job opportunities and feeling isolated are often big problems in rural areas. In 2001, depression and suicide among British farmers rose dramatically when a huge outbreak of foot and mouth disease forced many of them to kill their animals.

Some studies have shown that people in ethnic minority groups may get depressed more than others – possibly because they feel cut off from their culture and home country. For example, Asian women living in the USA seem to be more at risk than white women. However, there are other factors, too. Many people from ethnic minorities are poorer and have more problems to deal with than the white majority.

High levels of unemployment and poverty, for example on this US Navajo-Hopi Indian reservation, may be partly responsible for increasing depression in certain societies.

Depression also seems less common among people with 'traditional' hunting or farming lifestyles, who live in small, close-knit communities. Instances of depression among native people in Australia, the USA and Canada used to be very rare. Nowadays, however, traditional lifestyles have mostly disappeared, and depression is rising faster in these groups than among the white population.

Who suffers from depression?

When can depression strike? Many doctors still mistakenly see depression as an adult's disease. However, cases of depression among the young are on the increase. Children can sometimes suffer depression because of parents pressuring them to do well at school, or because of bullying, abuse, or problems with drink or drugs. Until their teens, boys are more likely than girls to suffer from depression. When they are older, however, females seem to get depressed around twice as often as males. However, these statistics may not show the whole picture, as boys are often more embarrassed than girls to admit how they feel. In a 2001 survey by the international support group Samaritans, about 20 per cent of young people said they would laugh at a male friend if he said he was depressed. It is possible that boys' depression may be 'masked', coming out instead in violence, theft, drug-taking or heavy drinking.

Depression seems to hit hardest among the middle-aged. People in this age group may have to deal with problems such as job stress or divorce. They may feel there is nothing left to look forward to. Elderly people often become depressed, too. They may have to cope with the death of a husband or wife, sickness, pain, and no longer being able to look after themselves.

ff When he was four or five he would make comments like, 'The playground's a lonely place,' and, 'You'd be better off if I'd never been born.'

(Social worker, Lindy Garnette, talking on CNN about her depressed fourteen-year-old son Ben)

Depression in developing countries

Nearly all research into depression has been done in rich Western countries. But 80 per cent of the world's population lives – often in very difficult conditions – in **developing countries**. Experts believe that most depressed people are probably living in the Third World, where there are very few trained **psychiatrists**, and most people cannot afford to buy **antidepressants**. It is thought that only around 5 per cent of depression sufferers in Africa and China get any medical treatment.

This Ugandan boy is infected with HIV.

HIV and depression

In Uganda one person in ten is **HIV**-positive and nearly every family has been affected by HIV/AIDS. Researchers found that 24 per cent of Ugandans now suffer from depression – more than four times the highest rate in Western countries. Depressed people often stop caring about themselves. Research shows that many Ugandans have started to do risky things, such as driving very fast and dangerously, or having unprotected sex (not using a condom). Practising unprotected sex will almost certainly increase the spread of HIV – creating a vicious circle in which depression will become even more widespread.

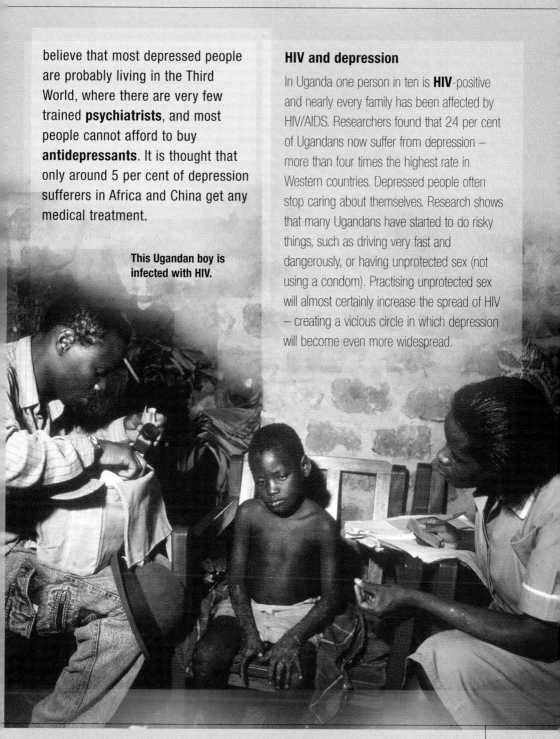

What causes depression?

The fact that depression is described as a 'mental' illness can be rather confusing. Depression is very often a **physical** illness – like **diabetes**, for example. While diabetes is caused by lack of **insulin** in the **pancreas**, depression is usually caused by a low level of mood-related chemicals in the brain, called **neurotransmitters**. It is the *symptoms* of depression that are mental, or in the mind.

The three main factors related to depression are physical (to do with our bodies), **psychological** (to do with the mind) and social (to do with the people around us). The root of a person's depression can include more than one of these factors at the same time.

Physical factors

Nearly all depression is linked to a low level of neurotransmitters in the brain. Neurotransmitters pass messages between the brain cells that control our moods. Levels of neurotransmitters can fall for many reasons. This may make people feel terrible, even if everything in their life seems to be going well, and can explain why some people's depression seems to have no obvious cause.

On-going problems, such as having constant arguments with a loved one or losing a job, can produce stress chemicals in a person's body. These can lower the level of neurotransmitters in the brain, making a short-term, 'understandable' depression difficult to shake off. Some physical illnesses also affect our levels of neurotransmitters. Examples are strokes and Parkinson's disease, and some infectious diseases such as glandular fever.

Seasonal **affective disorder** (SAD) is another type of physical depression. SAD is caused by lack of sunlight during short, dark winter days. Sunlight contains ultraviolet (UV) light. If people do not get enough UV light, their brains may start to produce a lot of **melatonin** – the same chemical that makes animals such as bears go into hibernation. There are around 10 million SAD sufferers in the northern USA, but their mood improves by springtime when the days start to get longer.

Alcohol and illegal drugs such as cocaine can also affect a person's brain chemistry, either causing depression or making it worse. Many depressed people, especially men, use drugs or alcohol to lift their mood for a while. However, they may become **addicted**, needing more of the substance to make them feel better – and feeling worse each time the effects wear off. Some legal, medical drugs can act as depressants, too, for example drugs for high blood pressure and arthritis pain relievers.

What causes depression?

Psychological factors

The **psychological** causes of depression may be 'understandable', for example the death of someone close, or breaking up with a boyfriend or girlfriend. Nearly everyone will go through a natural period of grieving or recovery in these situations. However, people who already have a chemical imbalance in their brains may develop major depressive disorder (see page 8).

People with serious or terminal illnesses, such as cancer or heart disease, often suffer from depression as they come to terms with their illness and face the possibility of dying. Depression is also quite common among people suffering from **post-traumatic stress disorder**, a condition that may develop after someone has been attacked or gone through a major disaster such as an earthquake. Post-traumatic depression may not set in until months or even years after a traumatic event.

Post-traumatic depression

In 2002, some British health authorities said they were finding it hard to provide enough mental health support to people from war-torn countries such as Bosnia-Herzegovina, who were trying to settle in the UK. Even several years after the war had ended, many refugees were still suffering from very severe post-traumatic depression – caused by the stress of trying to survive in a dangerous war zone and seeing many people being killed.

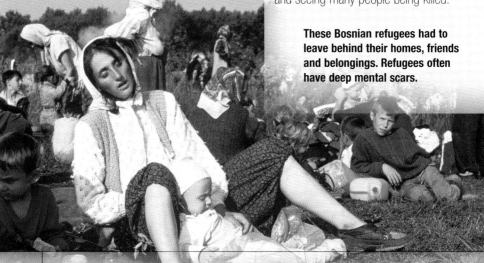

These Bosnian refugees had to leave behind their homes, friends and belongings. Refugees often have deep mental scars.

Social factors

Scientists believe that some people may even 'learn' to be depressed by copying the behaviour of people around them. For example, children whose parents are always depressed may grow up thinking it is normal to see everything in a negative light and to expect the worst in every situation. They are sometimes described as the kind of people who always see a glass as being half-empty rather than half-full.

Some people may develop **cognitive distortions** (fixed, negative ideas). For example, an attractive person may be totally convinced that he or she is ugly or a 'bad person'. If people do well in school, they may think it is because the teacher feels sorry for them – not because they deserved good marks!

❝When I get depressed I tend to eat. It's hard to feel good about yourself when you are depressed ... but who has the energy to spare to begin an exercise programme? I spend so much energy just getting through the day.❞

(Lisa-Marie, a depressed teenager)

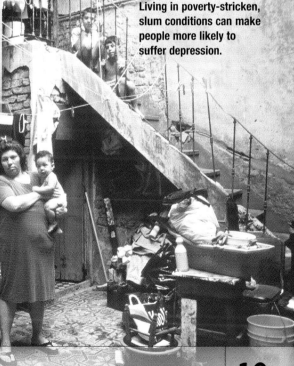

Living in poverty-stricken, slum conditions can make people more likely to suffer depression.

Living with depression

Daniel's story

When he was 24, Daniel Levy, a young British lawyer, was hit by depression. Daniel soon found that he could no longer concentrate on anything. He had to leave his job and stayed in bed for months. 'Later I became convinced I had committed a terrible crime, and that the police were hunting me down,' he says. Although he did not realize it, Daniel had **manic depression**. Daniel thinks an underlying chemical imbalance in his brain may have been triggered by stress.

Daniel started to read the Christian Bible and seeing 'great insights' into the scriptures. Religious obsessions are quite common among manic depressives. 'I ended up doing something so embarrassing I still can't bear to talk about it,' he says. 'I was arrested and sent to a **psychiatric** hospital. It was full of people with all sorts of mental diseases, which was quite frightening because I still didn't believe that I really was ill.'

When he is depressed, Daniel finds it hard to get up in the mornings. He has not been able to hold down a full-time job since he first became ill.

Daniel has attempted to commit **suicide** twice. 'I don't think I really wanted to die,' he says. 'I was just incredibly tired and desperate to sleep. My parents found me both times, and I would never do it again because of the pain it would cause them.'

Now 44, Daniel has been on mood-stabilizing drugs for years, but says he hardly ever feels totally 'normal'. 'More than anything I have to be careful not to get over-excited, because that could spark another episode of mania. Being manic can be very frightening. On the one hand you can imagine you are the president, but at the same time you can be convinced there is a plot to kill you. I have been lucky because my friends and family have stood by me.'

Today, Daniel works as an educator for the UK mental health charity SANE, trying to increase public understanding about manic depression. He hopes this will eventually make life easier for other sufferers.

The chemical brain

Our moods are controlled by very sensitive chemicals in our brains, called **neurotransmitters**. Scientists admit that they are far from fully understanding how these chemicals work. However, we do know that depression is often caused when, for some reason, our brains do not produce enough neurotransmitters.

A sense of meaning

The part of the brain where these chemicals work on our moods is the frontal lobe. Among other things, the frontal lobe brings together our conscious and unconscious minds to give a feeling of 'meaning' to our thoughts and emotions. For example, people who have an injury to their frontal lobe often lose the ability to understand the punch-lines of jokes – they can no longer find the humour funny.

When people are depressed, they often say that life seems to have lost all 'meaning' or pattern. It seems to have become just a chain of pointless events, where everything is falling apart. Depression sufferers can no longer find enjoyment in things that used to be fun and 'mean something' to them.

On the other hand, **manic depressives** going through manic periods – which can last for weeks or months – see great meaning in even the most ordinary events. For them, everything seems perfectly ordered, crystal-clear and linked together.

The brain's frontal lobes, involved in controlling our emotions, are shown here in pink.

> **❝I knew that if anybody spoke to me or looked at me too closely, the tears would fly out of my eyes and the sobs would fly out of my throat and I'd cry for a week. I could feel the tears brimming and sloshing in me like water in a glass that is unsteady and too full.❞**
>
> (US author Sylvia Plath in her famous novel about depression, *The Bell Jar*)

Defective genes

Scientists at the Royal Ottawa Hospital, in Canada, have found a faulty **gene** in severely depressed and **suicidal** patients. The gene affects the production of a neurotransmitter, called **serotonin**, in their brains. It is hoped that one day scientists will be able to develop **gene therapy** to remove or repair such defective genes, removing the underlying cause for many people's depression. Another possibility is that they could develop a test to spot faulty genes and identify people most at risk of depression, so they can get early treatment.

Hormones and depression

Some cases of depression seem to be linked to chemicals in our bodies called **hormones**. Hormones control a person's growth and development. Some of the most important ones are the sex hormones **testosterone** (in males) and **oestrogen** (in females). Men have a fairly constant level of testosterone in their bodies until they grow old. However, a woman's levels of oestrogen and other sex hormones are constantly changing. This may help to explain why, from **puberty** onwards, women seem to suffer from depression more than men.

A woman's hormone levels rise and fall during her monthly **menstrual cycle** (between periods), when she is pregnant and again at the **menopause**, which happens around the age of 45–55. During the menopause, a woman's periods stop for good and the levels of oestrogen in her body fall to a fraction of their previous levels. This sudden drop in oestrogen levels may cause depression in some women. Many women also feel depressed, emotional or grouchy just before their period – this is one of the symptoms of **pre-menstrual syndrome (PMS)**.

A new baby – cause for joy or depression?

After giving birth, a woman's hormonal levels fall quickly. Many people expect a new mother to be full of joy about the new baby. However, on top of the hormonal changes, a new mother usually feels very tired, and is faced with the huge responsibility of looking after a helpless baby. All these factors may add up to make her feel trapped and depressed.

About half of all women suffer from the '**baby blues**', which makes them feel quite low for a few days after birth. Between 5 and 20 per cent will go on to suffer **post-natal depression**, which normally sets in within a few weeks of the birth. Babies with mothers suffering from post-natal depression may develop more slowly than other babies. They may learn to speak at a later age, have sleep problems, cry more and smile less often. One or two women in every 1000 will develop a condition called post-natal **psychosis**. They will suffer from **hallucinations** and **delusions**, and in very severe cases they may end up hurting or even killing themselves or the baby.

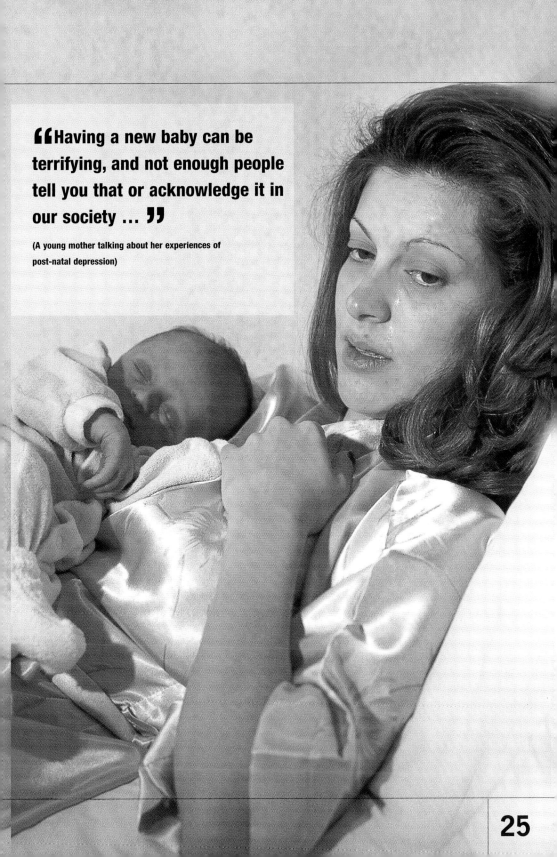

"Having a new baby can be terrifying, and not enough people tell you that or acknowledge it in our society ... "

(A young mother talking about her experiences of post-natal depression)

Depression and genius

People with depression – especially **manic depression** – are often extremely talented and creative. They may be able to use the energy of their illness to achieve fame and fortune, or be inspired by their suffering to produce great works of art. Some of our most brilliant actors, artists, politicians and musicians have been manic depressives. Famous examples include the authors Leo Tolstoy and Charles Dickens, the composer Beethoven, the actor Robert Downey Jr. and the rock star Axl Rose.

During manic episodes, the levels of **neurotransmitters** in a manic depressive person's brain shoot up way above normal. This means the sufferer may have huge amounts of energy and need less sleep. During this period a manic-depressive person might feel intensely happy and confident and take daredevil risks. It is possible to track the mood swings of one manic depressive, the German composer Robert Schumann, from his musical output. He composed nothing at all during 1844, a period of severe depression. However, he wrote an incredible 27 pieces of music during a manic episode in 1849. Today, the mood swings of manic depression can usually be kept under control with drugs, but many sufferers find they miss the 'highs', when they had boundless energy and felt they could achieve anything.

The US comedian Richard Pryor was renowned for making other people laugh – but in his own life he often suffered from alcohol and drug abuse and very bad depression.

> **❝I was handing in essays that made no sense whatsoever, and because I was manic I thought they were brilliant. I'd receive a mark of 28 per cent for an essay that was barely written in sentences and assume it was a typing error.❞**
>
> (Former student, Rachael Tooth, talking about her experiences with manic depression while at university)

Misery and art

Many famous people also suffer from **unipolar disorder** (see page 9), ranging from Jim Carrey and Elton John to Janet Jackson and Queen Elizabeth II. The misery of depression has actually been an inspiration in many cases, for example for the songs of Nirvana's Kurt Cobain and the novels and poems of Sylvia Plath. However, people with unipolar disorder do not usually have such intense periods of energy and output as those with manic depression. They too often find it difficult or impossible to work during a really bad bout of depression.

The 19th-century artist, Vincent van Gogh, famously cut off his own ear during a bout of severe depression.

Depression and young people

For many young people, being a teenager feels like being on an emotional roller-coaster ride. Teenagers can feel angry, miserable and misunderstood. Parents often laugh this off as 'teenage **angst**' – a phase that their children will outgrow. Even expert **psychologists** believed, until recently, that young people could not actually become depressed. We now know that this is not true.

Although depression is probably less common in young people than in adults, the American Academy of Child and Adolescent **Psychiatry** estimates that 3.4 million young people in the USA could be suffering from this condition. **Suicide** figures are one clear piece of evidence of youth depression. In the USA, around twelve young people kill themselves each day. In many Western countries the suicide rate has tripled since the 1970s, and only traffic accidents account for more youth deaths.

The diagnosis problem

It is still difficult to know for sure just how common depression is among young people. Often the illness is not diagnosed correctly. This may be because some doctors still do not believe that young people can suffer from depression. Signs of depression may also be missed because depressed teenagers tend to

Feeling 'left out' or being bullied at school can lead some young people to feel depressed.

behave quite differently from depressed adults, being violent, angry or rude. Teenagers themselves may not realize there is anything wrong with them, thinking it is 'normal' to feel miserable all the time.

People with eating disorders are often also depressed.

Youth depression is often linked to big problems, such as coming from a broken home or being bullied at school. However, television and magazines may also be partly to blame. Teenagers can be very heavily influenced by the media. On screen, life nearly always seems exciting and full of beautiful people. This can make the reality of a teenager's own life seem depressingly dull. On top of this, many parents put pressure on their children to do well at school. Children who do not meet these high expectations may feel they have let other people – or themselves – down.

The media link

Scientists at Harvard University found that the eating disorder **anorexia** – which is often linked to depression – became much more common among teenage girls in Fiji after US-style TV programmes arrived on the island. Traditionally, dieting was unknown in Fiji and thin women were seen as weak. However, within three years of getting televisions, 74 per cent of girls said that they felt 'too big' or 'fat' and 15 per cent were regularly making themselves sick to lose weight.

Why is depression on the increase?

Depression has been increasing rapidly since the Second World War, and is striking people at a younger age with each generation that passes. No one is entirely sure why this is the case. Some experts feel that in some ways life today can be much more stressful than it was a few hundred years ago. Most people then could expect to live their whole lives in the same village, doing the same job, surrounded by people they knew well.

Loss of security

Today we have far more opportunities – but life is changing at a faster pace, and this can make people feel frightened and insecure. Their jobs may take them far away from their friends and families, or they may worry about problems such as unemployment and crime. People worry more about world issues, such as terrorism, **climate change** and scientific developments, such as cloning. Some people find it difficult to imagine what our world may be like in another 50 years' time. For many people, the world is changing too quickly, making them feel anxious and depressed. People today are also living longer than before. Elderly people often suffer from depression, and this accounts for some of the rise in depression statistics.

Over-diagnosis?

Some experts suggest that the increase in reported depression cases may also be partly due to over-diagnosis. People are slowly learning that depression is curable and is nothing to be ashamed about.

This means they are more willing to seek treatment – especially as **antidepressants** are now safer and more effective than ever before. Many of these people are genuinely depressed. However, prescriptions for antidepressants rose by more than 700 per cent between 1990 and 1999 – much faster than depression could really have increased. Just as many people think they have 'flu when they only have a cold, many people think they are depressed if they just have a temporary attack of the blues. Most doctors know that many cases of depression go unnoticed. It is therefore possible that some doctors may prescribe antidepressants even if the patient does not match enough symptoms on the checklist (see page 6). Their patients feel miserable and they want them to feel better. However, this could be dangerous. Antidepressants change the chemistry of the brain, and it is not known what long-term effects this could have for people whose levels of **neurotransmitters** are not actually unbalanced in the first place.

In the weeks and months following the terrorist attacks in New York on 11 September 2001, many people all around the world suffered from shock, **post-traumatic stress disorder** and depression.

Does depression run in families?

It is possible that a tendency for depression can be passed on in the genes from a parent to their child.

Scientists believe that, in many cases, our chances of developing depression may be written in our **genes**. Genes are strands of information inside our bodies' cells. They are passed on from parents to their children and control every aspect about how our bodies will develop – for example hair colour or nose shape. Some genes may also make us more likely to develop certain diseases.

Genes for depression

Some people receive faulty genes, which tell their brains to produce only very low levels of **neurotransmitters**. These people may be much more likely to develop depression, especially if they go through a rough patch or emotional problem. There is a strong genetic link for **manic depression**, which on average affects one person in every 100. If a person's parent is a manic depressive, he or she has a one in five chance of developing the illness. If both parents have the condition, the risk is more like one in two. **Unipolar disorder** (see page 9) does not have such a strong genetic link. However, the children of people with depression are still three times more likely to be affected than people in the population at large. This may be partly due to the effect of living with depressed parents.

A scientific challenge

Around 50,000 genes are thought to be responsible for the development of the brain. It may take many years to identify the specific genes linked to depression. It is important to remember, however, that no one is doomed to suffer from depression, regardless of his or her genes. They may just be more likely to develop the illness.

Even if a person's identical twin – who has exactly the same genetic make-up – suffers from depression, the risk for the other twin is not 100 per cent, but around 70 per cent. This shows that there are other factors apart from genetics involved in developing depression. A person's way of coping with his or her particular problems has a big impact, too.

Background photograph: Scientists are beginning to unlock the secret information contained in our genes, which are found on chromosomes such as these.

Depression and suicide

Around 15 per cent of depression sufferers end up taking their own lives – most often those who have not sought treatment. They just cannot see any end to their misery and feel that **suicide** is the only way to put a stop to their suffering. In 2001, around one million people worldwide committed suicide – one person every 40 seconds. In the USA, more people die from suicide than from murder.

Women are three times more likely than men to attempt to commit suicide. However, men are more likely to succeed. This is because men often use more violent means, such as shooting or hanging themselves. Many women take overdoses of painkillers, and can often be treated in hospital if found in time.

Some depressed young people take an overdose of pills because they feel angry and want to 'make someone sorry'. Sadly, many of them cannot be saved in time and do die.

The explosion in youth suicide

Youth suicide rates in Western countries have risen rapidly since the 1970s. This is partly because young people, especially young men, are often less likely than adults to get treatment for depression, because they may be frightened or embarrassed. People who bottle up their feelings are more likely to end up feeling hopeless and suicidal than people who talk things through with a friend, family member or counsellor.

A cry for help

Parasuicide (where a person may take an overdose and then call the emergency services, or carry out the act in a place where they hope they will be found) is also common among young people. These acts are often called 'cries for help' and are committed by people who do not feel they have any other way to make people pay attention to how bad they are feeling. People who have attempted suicide once will probably feel very depressed and guilty about it, and are quite likely to make another attempt. These people are most likely to repeat a suicide attempt during the first three months, although they may be at risk for several years.

Warning signs

It may be very difficult to tell if someone is feeling suicidal. However, experts say that warning signs include a person saying things like, 'I won't be seeing you again,' or, 'I won't be a problem for you much longer.' Suicidal people may also give up regular activities, suddenly do badly at school or work and keep away from friends. They may give or throw away favourite possessions or important belongings.

35

Tackling depression

People with a disease such as scurvy (caused by lack of vitamins) will get better if they eat fresh fruit to boost the body's level of vitamin C. In the same way, a person with depression will usually improve by taking medicines called **antidepressants**, which restore the balance of **neurotransmitters** in his or her brain. Other treatments are also effective, including 'talking therapies' such as counselling or therapies based around art or music.

Fear of treatment

Sadly, however, many people still do not get treatment. They may think that having depression means they are going 'mad', or that they will be locked away in a **psychiatric** hospital. In fact, people are usually only hospitalized in very severe cases. Many people think that depression is something that happens to 'other people'. They may only visit their doctor when they start to experience **physical** symptoms, such as **insomnia**, weight loss, headaches or panic attacks.

The mind-body link

It may seem strange that depression, an illness of the mind, can have physical effects like this. However, a person's state of mind can have a big effect on their physical health. Depression also lowers sufferers' immune systems, making them more open to illnesses such as colds and flu.

People with untreated depression often find it difficult to hold down a 'normal' life, and have a higher than average chance of ending up homeless, unemployed, **addicted** to drink or drugs, or in prison. A child with depression may fail at school and have difficulties getting on with others, always feeling like an outsider.

Chances of success

Treatment is more successful if it is started early. If a person has got to the point of being determined to commit **suicide**, it may take a long time to help him or her get back to normal. Early treatment can dramatically reduce the risk of the depression returning. Half of all people who are treated for a depressive illness will never have another episode. Very few people who have a second episode will go on to have a third.

Tackling depression

Plans for the future

To encourage sufferers to come forward, governments around the world must educate the public about depression. Sadly, however, the World Health Organization (WHO) says that around one quarter of the world's countries still have no laws or plans to deal with the illness. The WHO wants governments to make **antidepressants** more widely available and provide public education to remove the embarrassment surrounding depression. It is also calling for better training for doctors to help them recognize the illness in its early stages. Programmes dealing with issues linked to depression, such as poverty, unemployment, racism, bullying and child abuse, are also important.

Progress has already been made in many areas. The American **Psychiatric** Association has run depression screening and information days since 1991. So far, more than 100,000 people have come forward to be tested for depression. The US Surgeon General also set up the country's first **suicide** prevention strategy in May 2001. Australian authorities launched their first mental health strategy in 1992, and have produced a comic called *Blue Daze* to educate young people about depression. The UK government has set up special hotlines for young men in areas of high male unemployment, where depression and suicide rates are rising. Talking problems through is one of the most important first steps in dealing with depression.

For some sufferers, anonymous counselling services can be an important lifeline.

Depression in the lab

Scientists are researching new treatments for depression, for example transcranial magnetic stimulation (TMS) to help severely depressed people. TMS involves sending magnetic impulses into the brain to try to 'jog' it back into producing a normal level of **neurotransmitters**.

Special brain imaging techniques may help scientists to literally 'see' depression on a computer screen, showing up the chemical activity in a person's brain in different colours. This could make it easier to diagnose people at risk, and to keep an eye on how well a patient's drug treatment is working.

Scientists are even trying to grow healthy brain cells on microchips. It is hoped these could be inserted into depressed people's brains to 'mend' their faulty electrochemical systems.

Scientists are looking into many areas of depression – for example finding out how stress levels may affect brain chemistry.

Tackling depression

Dealing with depressed friends or relatives

People often do not know how to deal with depressed friends or relatives. They may become frustrated or even angry, feeling that the sufferer is wallowing in self-pity and should be trying harder to be more positive. Well-meaning advice such as, 'Pull yourself together,' or, 'Come on, snap out of it,' does not help. If sufferers could just shrug off the depression they would have already done it! Friends and relatives may start to avoid the sufferer, because his or her low mood is draining and brings them down. This can make the sufferer feel even more alone and isolated.

Even though it may seem almost impossible to help or 'get through' to a depressed person, sufferers are often unable to recover alone and depend greatly on the people around them.

Love and support

So how can a depressed person be helped? First of all, the sufferer needs to be told that he or she is loved, no matter what – many depression sufferers feel that their situation is hopeless. The person may be comforted by being told that he or she is almost definitely going to get better, no matter how bad things seem at the time.

Depressed people should be encouraged to do as much as they can for themselves. However, if it all seems too much for the sufferer, it is helpful to do practical things for them, such as shopping or cleaning. At times sufferers may even feel too exhausted to get up or wash themselves.

Health professionals say it is important to get help quickly if a person's situation deteriorates rapidly – for example if they talk a lot about feeling guilty, wanting to end their life, or if they stop eating or drinking.

People looking after depressed relatives need help, too. It is often a lonely, difficult and tiring job. They may sometimes even end up getting depressed themselves, and start to feel it is somehow their fault that the sick person is not getting any better.

It is important that carers give themselves a break every now and again. Getting in touch with a local support group can also be a big help. These groups can put people in touch with others going through similar problems.

Legal matters

Unlike people with **physical** illnesses, people with mental illnesses such as depression can be treated against their will. This happens only in severe cases, if doctors think the sufferer is likely to harm themselves or someone else. A patient may be sent to a **psychiatric** hospital for anything from a few days to a year. Patients can appeal against the doctors' decision, but the process may take several weeks.

Losing a child

A mother with very serious depression may have her children taken away and put into foster care if the courts feel she cannot care for them properly. Once children have been taken away, it may be difficult for a parent to prove that he or she is well enough to care for their children. In making a decision, the courts' top concern is the welfare of the child. The feelings of older children may also be taken into account in deciding where they will live.

The cost of care

Another big legal issue facing depressed people is medical insurance. Many companies believe that mentally ill people will need a lot of costly psychiatric treatment, and either charge them much higher premiums than usual, or will not provide cover at all. The US Mental Health Equitable Treatment Act (2001) ruled that health insurance companies should stop doing this. However, some people still find they are being overcharged – even if they only suffered from one small bout of depression many years ago. This is not the case in countries with free healthcare, such as the UK.

Severely ill patients may be placed in a psychiatric ward for some time if doctors feel this is the best way of helping them to get better.

Discrimination in the workplace

People with depression can face legal problems at work, too. Many employers will not employ depressed people, or may sack them if they find out about their illness. Employers want their firms to make a lot of money, and may feel a depressed person is more likely to take time off sick. However, a special US government committee has been set up to look into problems in the workplace for people with all kinds of disabilities. In 2000, the committee spent US$200,000 (£138,000) on creating jobs for people suffering from mental illnesses.

Hiding the illness

A survey in 2002 by the British Mental Health Foundation found that two-thirds of people who have suffered from any kind of mental illness will not tell their employer. Many people said they were frightened they may be fired, would not be promoted, or that fellow workers would find out about the illness and treat them differently.

43

Treatment and counselling

Drug treatment

Without treatment, depression usually goes away by itself within about nine months. With **antidepressants**, however, around 70 per cent of patients get better in as little as three weeks. Women and people with milder depression respond best to this form of treatment.

However, the human mind is very complex, and the reasons for developing and recovering from depression may vary from person to person. This means scientists are still not sure exactly how antidepressants work. Some trials have even shown that the drugs themselves have very little effect, and that people actually 'cure' themselves, simply because they believe the drugs will work. Whether they are truly effective or not, antidepressants give many patients a 'breathing space' from their illness, giving them the energy to work out some of their problems. However, it may take a few weeks before a sufferer feels that his or her condition is improving, and the drugs must be taken for several more months after the sufferer feels better. If not, the depression can return even worse than before.

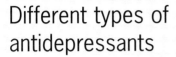

Different types of antidepressants

There are a variety of antidepressants. A person's doctor may advise him or her to try a range of brands until one is found that seems to work best. Today's major drugs belong to three groups: tricyclic antidepressants, selective **serotonin** reuptake inhibitors (SSRIs) and monoamine oxidase inhibitors (MAOIs). They all work to boost or maintain the brain's level of **neurotransmitters**.

The most famous SSRI is Prozac, which is one of the biggest selling drugs of all time. At least 40 million people around the world have taken it since it was launched in the late 1980s.

Unlike the old-fashioned drugs used for depression 50 years ago, such as pep pills and tranquillizers (which made a person very calm and sleepy), modern antidepressants are not **addictive**. However, some patients can suffer side effects, ranging from stomach bleeding to **insomnia** (see page 46). This is why it is very important to take antidepressants under the care of a doctor.

Side effects

Tricyclics were first developed in the late 1950s. These early drugs sometimes made people's mouths very dry and gave them blurred vision, but today these side effects are less common. Monoamine oxidase inhibitors (MAOIs) can sometimes react dangerously with foods such as cheese or avocado, causing high blood pressure and heart attacks. For this reason they are rarely used now, except for people who do not respond to other drugs. Selective **serotonin** reuptake inhibitors (SSRIs) usually do not have dangerous reactions with other medications, are difficult to overdose on, and have fewer side effects than other **antidepressants** – although they may cause nausea, headaches, diarrhoea and sleeping problems.

Manic depression is usually treated using long-term doses of lithium carbonate, a salt that occurs naturally in small amounts in our food. As a drug, lithium carbonate can help to stabilize a person's moods. It is important to have regular blood tests and drink plenty of water to make sure the level of lithium carbonate in the body is neither too low nor dangerously high. The possible side effects of this treatment may include weight gain and uncontrollable shaking.

Other options

For people with severe depression that does not improve after taking antidepressants, another option is electroconvulsive therapy (ECT). Electric shocks are sent into the brain through special pads attached to the patient's head while he or she is under general anaesthetic. No one is quite sure how ECT works, but it does seem helpful. However, side effects may include short-term memory loss and aches and pains, because the treatment can make a patient's body jump around a lot.

Counselling

Since depression usually has both **physical** and **psychological** causes, the best kind of treatment is often a mixture of drugs and 'talking therapies'. Just talking and being listened to can be a big help to people with depression.

There are many different kinds of talking therapy and it is important that people find out which method suits them best.

One type of therapy is counselling, in which the depression sufferer can talk through their problems and feelings. During counselling and psychotherapy sessions, sufferers also look into their own pasts to try to understand how and why their depression began.

Counsellors help people to get to the root causes of their problems and put them in perspective so they can get on with their lives.

Cognitive behavioural therapy (CBT)

Another kind of talking therapy is called cognitive behavioural therapy (CBT). As we have seen (see page 19), many depressed people have very low self-esteem and a fixed, negative way of thinking, called a **cognitive distortion**, for example believing they are bad people, boring, or ugly. CBT can help people to 'unlearn' their irrational way of thinking. CBT may include learning relaxation techniques, communication skills and assertiveness training.

Meditation can be a big help in overcoming depression.

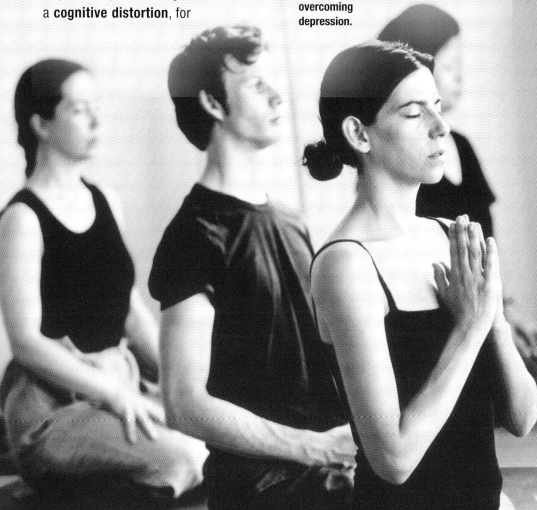

Complementary therapy

Today, alternative medicine is becoming more and more popular. Even though today's **antidepressants** are generally safe and have few side effects, some people do not want to use strong medical drugs to alter their brain's chemistry. They may prefer to use what they see as more natural and gentle treatments. St John's Wort is a herb that has been shown in some tests to work as well as Prozac. St John's Wort has become very popular as a natural antidepressant in the past few years. However, it can have some side effects and react dangerously with other medicines.

Studies have been carried out on some other alternative therapies, which also seem to have some effect on depression. These include **acupuncture**, **aromatherapy**, massage, **art therapy** and **music therapy**, and **meditation**. However, it is not always clear if these really 'work' themselves, or if the sufferer feels better simply because he or she is taking time to pamper him or herself.

Boosts to lift the spirits

Simple things such as listening to music, playing with a pet, taking a walk, having a hot bath and eating well can also alleviate the symptoms of depression – at least temporarily. Many depressed people do not have the energy to cook properly and eat only junk food, which can make them feel more tired and ill. Exercise, meanwhile, makes the brain release chemicals called **endorphins**, which can make people feel happier for a short while.

Seasonal **affective disorder** (SAD) is a type of depression caused in winter by lack of sunlight (see page 16). The best treatment for this seems to be phototherapy, which involves sitting in front of bright ultraviolet lights.

> **❝I found that exercise helped. One thing I did was to get straight out of bed and go for a brisk half-hour walk.❞**
>
> **(Australian actor Garry McDonald, who suffered from panic disorder and depression)**

People to talk to

It may seem very simple, but talking is one of the best ways of dealing with depression. Talking things through can often make it easier to find a way of solving problems or coming to terms with difficult situations. People who keep everything bottled up may become more and more convinced that their situation is hopeless.

Many depression sufferers feel that it is difficult or embarrassing to speak to people who know them, such as parents or friends. There are many professional groups that will listen in confidence to depressed people. Counsellors will take the person and his or her feelings and problems seriously. Counsellors can often also help in

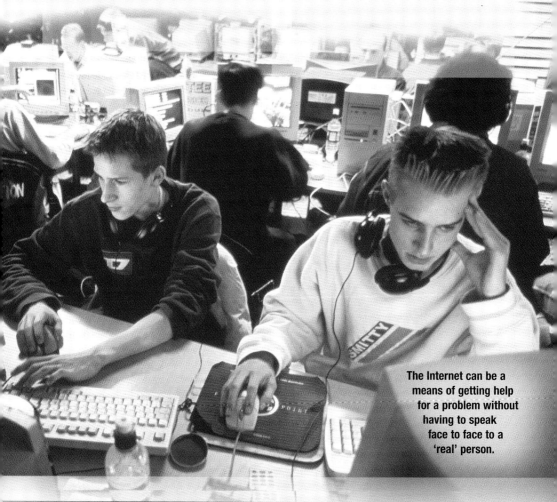

The Internet can be a means of getting help for a problem without having to speak face to face to a 'real' person.

dealing with problems such as revising for exams or making friends at a new school. However, they may contact emergency services if they think the sufferer is so depressed that he or she might attempt to commit **suicide**.

Helplines

Helplines are available 24-hours a day to provide support for people going through a crisis. As the conversations are anonymous, these services are often used by people who do not feel ready to talk to a doctor, **psychiatrist**, counsellor or therapist.

Help on the web

Many organizations have email counselling services. Teenagers may feel happier getting help via the Internet rather than face to face. The Samaritans' website even has a button that can be clicked to make the Samaritans' logo disappear. This means that, in a public place such as an Internet café, no one will realize the person is using a counselling service.

One of the worst things for depressed people is feeling that they are alone. Sharing thoughts and experiences with other people who are in the same situation can be a big help. There are many online chat rooms and discussion boards on all issues that affect teenagers. However, not everyone chatting on a website is as nice as they seem. No one should give out contact details or their address, or arrange to meet anyone from a chat room.

Schools

Many schools have special counsellors, who are trained to help young people going through various problems, including depression. If not, a trusted teacher can often offer a sympathetic ear, or at least give advice about how to find professional help.

Religious leaders

Religious leaders, such as priests or rabbis, can help, too. They may be able to give a more spiritual view of a person's problems and how they can be overcome. For some people, religious faith can be very comforting, helping a person to see problems as part of a 'bigger picture' and making some kind of sense of his or her personal difficulties.

Information and advice

The following organizations, websites and books can provide a huge amount of useful information about the causes of, and treatment for, depression.

Contacts in the UK

Befrienders
www.befrienders.org
This organization has links to 1700 crisis centres worldwide, and 31,000 volunteers working in 40 countries. It provides a 24-hour confidential telephone and email counselling service.

Child and Adolescent Bipolar Foundation (CABF)
www.cabf.org
The CABF has links on **manic depression**.

Depression Alliance
Tel: 020 7633 0557
www.depressionalliance.org
This is an organization run by sufferers to help others. Depression Alliance provides information on symptoms and treatment, and runs awareness-raising campaigns.

MIND
Tel: 020 8519 2122
www.mind.org.uk
MIND is a big charity working for carers and people suffering from mental health problems. The website provides a lot of information about depression and other illnesses.

Samaritans
Tel: 08457 909090,
www.samaritans.org.uk
The Samaritans offer a 24-hour listening service for the depressed or **suicidal**. The website also has an email counselling service.

Young Minds Information Service
Tel: 0800 0182138,
www.youngminds.org.uk
This organization provides information on depression, self-injury and mental health problems for parents and children.

Contacts in Ireland

Childline
Tel: 1-800-666666
A crisis line for young people going through problems such as abuse, homelessness or depression.

Samaritans
Tel: 1-850-609090
A 24-hour listening service for the depressed or suicical.

Contacts in the USA

National Child Abuse Hotline
Tel: 800/4-A-CHILD or 800/422-4453
This is a 24-hour counselling service for young people suffering from abuse.

The National Mental Health Association
www.nmha.org
The National Mental Health Association has stacks of information, and is the largest non-profit organization for mental health and illness in the USA.

National Youth Crisis Hotline
Tel: 800-HIT-HOME: 800/448-4663
This service aims to help any young person facing major problems such as drugs, crime, violence or contemplating suicide.

Contacts in Australia

The Australian National Depression Initiative

www.beyondblue.org.au
The website includes information, the stories of famous Australian sufferers and their recovery, and news about what the government is doing to tackle depression.

Kids' Helpline

Tel: 1-800-55-1800 or
www.kidshelp.com.au
This is a hotline for young people going through a crisis or feeling depressed.

Samaritans

Tel: 1-800-198313
This is a listening line for people feeling depressed or suicidal.

Contacts in Canada

Kids' Helpline

Tel: 1-800-668-6868
This is a hotline for young people going through a crisis or with any kind of problem.

Contacts in New Zealand

Samaritans

Tel: 04 473-9739
This is a 24-hour listening service for people who are depressed or suicidal.

Youthline

Tel: 0800 376-633
This is a telephone counselling service for anyone feeling emotionally distressed.

Further reading

The Bell Jar by Sylvia Plath; New York: Harper Perennial, 2000. Plath was a famous author who herself struggled with depression and finally committed suicide in 1963. The book describes a young woman's breakdown and treatment in a **psychiatric** institution.

Bipolar Disorder: A Guide for Patients and Families by Francis Mondimore; Baltimore: Johns Hopkins Press, 1999

The Catcher in the Rye by J.D. Salinger; London: Little, Brown and Co., reprinted 1991

Darkness Visible: A Memoir of Madness by William Styron; London: Vintage Books, 2001

Hand Me Down Blues by Dr Michael Yapko; New York: Griffin Trade Paperbacks, 2000

Helping Friends in Trouble: Stress, Depression and Suicide by Joyce Walker; Minnesota: University of Minnesota, revised 1995

Selected Poems by Anne Sexton; Boston: Mariner Books: 1999

Disclaimer
All the Internet addresses (URLs) given in this book were valid at the time of going to press. However, due to the dynamic nature of the Internet, some addresses may have changed, or sites may have changed or ceased to exist since publication. While the author and Publisher regret any inconvenience this may cause readers, no responsibility for any such changes can be accepted by either the author or the Publisher.

Glossary

acupuncture
a Chinese alternative therapy, which involves inserting fine steel needles into the skin along energy channels, called meridians

addicted, addictive
being dependent on a drug

affective disorder
another name for depression

angst
feelings of anger, fear and irritability

anorexia
an eating disorder where people are obsessed about their weight and starve themselves

antidepressant
a drug or agent that alleviates symptoms of depression

aromatherapy
an alternative therapy in which scented essential oils from plants and flowers are massaged into the body

art therapy
the use of art to allow depressed people to express their feelings and emotions

baby blues
a mild form of depression, common in women who have just given birth

bipolar disorder
another name for manic depression

climate change
a world wide change in weather patterns, possibly caused by the gradual warming of the planet by pollution

cognitive distortions
fixed, negative ideas

Communism
a political system in which all property is owned by the community and the government restricts personal liberty

delusions
false ideas or impressions, for example people with delusions may be convinced that someone is following or spying on them

developing countries
poor countries in the Third World, such as Ethiopia or India

diabetes
a disease caused when the body does not produce enough insulin

dysthmia
a mild form of depression that lasts for around two years

endorphins
chemicals released by the brain after an injury, or during exercise

gene therapy
a developing branch of medicine in which doctors may be able to 'switch off' or remove genes that may trigger certain illnesses

genes
information within body cells that determines a person's characteristics, for example, hair colour or nose shape. Genes are passed down to us from our parents.

hallucinations
seeing or hearing things that are not really there

HIV
Human Immunodeficiency Virus. HIV attacks and destroys the body's immune system.

hormones
chemicals produced in the body that regulate or stimulate growth and development

insomnia
inability to sleep properly

insulin
a hormone produced in the body to break down sugar

lobotomy
an operation carried out many years ago on some people with mental illnesses, in which the frontal lobe of the brain was detached from the rest of the brain

lunatic asylum
a type of psychiatric hospital used many years ago for people with mental illnesses

manic depression
a type of depression with alternating moods of elation and misery

meditation
a technique for calming the mind and reaching inner relaxation, in which people may chant or concentrate hard on an image or a thought

melancholia
an old word for sadness or depression

melatonin
a chemical in our bodies with various functions. In large quantities, it causes animals such as bears to go into hibernation during winter.

menopause
the time when a woman's monthly periods finally stop, usually around the age of 45–55

menstrual cycle
the monthly cycle of hormones in a woman's body before menopause

mood disorder
another name for depression

music therapy
the use of singing, listening to music and imagery to help relieve depression and express feelings and emotions

neurotransmitters
chemicals that act as 'messengers' between the cells of the brain

oestrogen
the female hormone responsible for a woman's sexual development

pancreas
a gland near the stomach that produces substances to break down food

parasuicide
when someone seems to go through the motions of committing suicide, but hopes to be found before they die. It is often seen as a cry for help.

physical
to do with the body

post-natal depression
a type of depression from which up to 20 per cent of new mothers suffer. This may be partly due to the level of hormones in their bodies falling very quickly after the birth.

post-traumatic stress disorder
a condition of mental stress that sometimes follows a traumatic event

pre-menstrual syndrome (PMS)
a condition from which many women suffer during the week before their monthly period. It can make them feel very grouchy or depressed.

psychiatrist, psychiatry
a doctor that specializes in treating diseases and problems of the mind. Psychiatry is the study of such illnesses.

psychoanalysis
a type of therapy in which the patient is helped to explore his or her unconscious feelings and to recognize repressed fears and anxieties

psychological, psychologist
to do with the mind

psychosis
a severe mental state, resulting in hallucinations and delusions, and irrational behaviour

puberty
the period during which adolescents reach sexual maturity and become capable of reproduction

serotonin
an important neurotransmitter that can affect our moods

sociologist
a scientist who studies development and change in human society

suicide, suicidal
the intentional killing of oneself

testosterone
a male hormone, responsible for a man's sexual development

unipolar disorder
another name for depression

Index

Titles in the *Need to Know* series include:

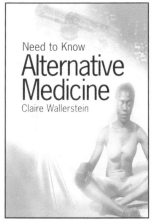

Need to Know
Alternative Medicine
Claire Wallerstein

Hardback   0 431 09808 5

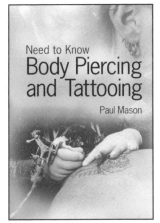

Need to Know
Body Piercing and Tattooing
Paul Mason

Hardback   0 431 09818 2

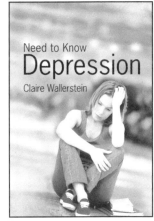

Need to Know
Depression
Claire Wallerstein

Hardback   0 431 09809 3

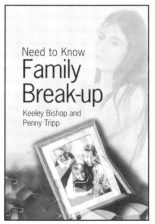

Need to Know
Family Break-up
Keeley Bishop and Penny Tripp

Hardback   0 431 09810 7

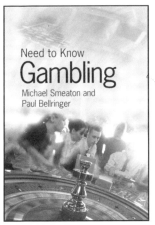

Need to Know
Gambling
Michael Smeaton and Paul Bellringer

Hardback   0 431 09819 0

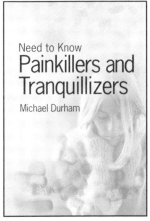

Need to Know
Painkillers and Tranquillizers
Michael Durham

Hardback   0 431 09811 5

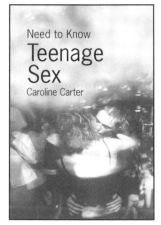

Need to Know
Teenage Sex
Caroline Carter

Hardback   0 431 09821 2

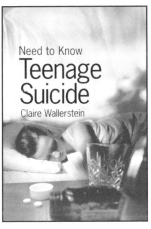

Need to Know
Teenage Suicide
Claire Wallerstein

Hardback   0 431 09820 4

Find out about the other titles in this series on our website www.heinemann.co.uk/library